S0-BNX-712

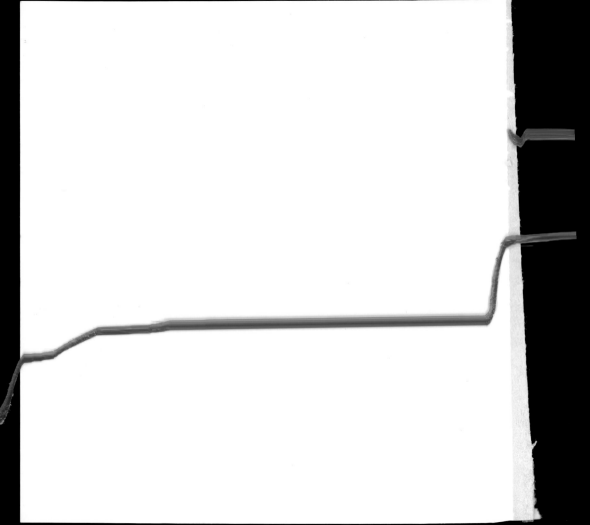

The Classified Cat

The Classified Cat

BY JOE DZIALO

illustrations by Kathy Piersall

Willow Creek® PRESS

Text © 2002 Joe Dzialo

Illustrations © 2002 Kathy Piersall/Blue Mountain Arts

Published by Willow Creek Press, P.O. Box 147, Minocqua, Wisconsin 54548

All rights reserved. No part of this book may be reproduced or transmitted in any form
by any means, electronic or mechanical, including photocopying, recording, or by any
information storage and retrieval system, without written permission from the Publisher.

Editor Andrea Donner
Art Director/Design Pat Linder

For information on other Willow Creek Press titles, call 1-800-850-9453

Library of Congress Cataloging-in-Publication Data
Dzialo, Joe, 1962-
The classified cat : a premier meeting-place for city felines / by Joe Dzialo
p. cm.
ISBN 1-57223-582-9 (hard : alk. paper)
1. Cats--Humor. 2. Personals--Humor I. Title.
PN6231.C23 D99 2002
741.5'973--dc21
2002008231

Printed in Canada

COMMON ABBREVIATIONS

M Male
F Female
D Divorced
S Single
G Gay
Bi Bisexual
L Lesbian
TG Transgendered
TS Transsexual
N Neutered
Sp Spayed
B Black
W White
Gr Gray
T Tabby
J Jewish
NS Nonsmoker

Dedicated to Martine, Charlotte, Cyprien, Shasha, and all New York City cats and their families.

—J.D.

STAR/TOP MODEL SMC, Morris the Cat double, my charm has taken me from stray-dom to stardom... seeks self aware FC for serious relationship, no one night stands, breed unimportant. Friends 1st. ☎ Call 16925

RESPECTABLE FC, pretty, silver-eyed petit Persian, 0' 8" seeks intellectual SMBC, 7-8, mating minded, well bred, white collar, clean. ✉ 113127

243 DATES AND STILL NO MR. RIGHT AND... unfortunately married to 3 Mr. Wrongs. Older optimistic, D cat, medium build, great teeth, nice legs seeks stable, solvent, sensual male for weekend getaways, Central Park, dinner, movies, etc....no plans for weekend? Call me Gramacy Park 39838930

PAVARATTI TO TUPAC.. Unique, one of a kind, street smart M cat. 9lbs. authentic Italian, slicked back hair, occasional goatee, works in sales, many interests, music buff, ISO self-respecting, SWF cat 3-7 yo, for moon-lite romantic drives down the FDR and more. H/W proportionate. Serious replies only. Brooklyn 4675654

WHO DO YOU LIKE...LETTERMAN OR LENO? M cat, 5, 12lbs, seeks F cuddle cat to watch late night TV. Must have cable and Tivo. Must share the remote. No channel surfing. Live in a + West Village 383789

TROUBLE IN GOTHAM CITY Hot GM cat, 6, 12lbs, cape crusader, seeks boy wonder in need of manly companionship. No fems or pretty boys. Looking for gladiator type for cruising downtown clubs."Holy jock straps Robin...could you be the guy!" Columbia U area. 9389300.

BOYFRIENDABLE Cute F. downtown kitty, semi punk, pierced, 3 yo, 6 lbs, seeks prof. cool cat to rock out with. Sense of humor a must. Starbucks first. East village 383789

MEOWA LISA FC, Tabby, work of art, mysterious, seeks the same... Is it your smile that attracts a lover? Then it will attract me. Send me your portrait with a note that will keep me in a daze for centuries. ✉ 09369

"I TAUT I TAW A PUDDY TAT" Our eyes met, you meowed, I purred, last Saturday (10/25) in the moonlite alley behind Dagastino's. Sufferin' succotash I'm in love. Call Sylvester ☎ 13125

The Classified Cat

KALEIDOSCOPIC YET WELL-BAL-ANCED Sexy, long legged, curvaceous, DF, 5 yo incurable romantic w. auburn locks, seeks single M prof cat, communicative, emotionally articulate for eternal soul-mate. Race unimportant. No couch clawers plse. All responses answered- ☎ ✉ Midtown 1438830

DESTINY CHILD-LIKE F CAT S black cat, 3 yo, lioness, fun, fit, flexible, ISO creative, monogamouse, self-supporting life partner. I need a 100% male cat who knows how to treat a female. Village 1438831

Great Purrsonality, Sexy SM Tabby, 5 yo, Big Chill era, looking for blue eyed F. burmese for discreet safe + sane erotic fun. My strength and stamina will fulfill all your wildest fantasies. Limits respected. NS Brooklyn. lv mess. ☎ 88467

DO YOU HAVE A BIG ONE? Heart that is...DFC,8 yo. European decent, not into singles scene...ISO emotionally secure MC for delectable mixture of compassion,honesty and companionship. No macho's. Meet for tea...NS Brooklyn. lv mess. ☎ 88468

COULD YOU BE THE ONE? I want to start this year on a positive note. Vivacious, long tail, blue eyed, J feline seeks a well balanced J male for possible LTR. No duds or neg.attitudes. ☎ All boroughs Riverside 1438832

OUT OF THE CLOSET. GM cat, 4, 9lbs, a bit shy but open minded looking to try something new with older, experienced M cat. You, clean fur, (non-shedding preferred), 5-13 yo. slim build, your place or mine. West Village 1438833

ONLY A-LIST CATS NEED APPLY. You- a mover and shaker, confident, pure breed, with contacts in the film industry. Me-2 yo, witty with blockbuster appeal and a Pamela Anderson figure- No phonies or wanna be's... The real deal only. Possible mutually satisfying relationship. Lets do lunch- LA/NYC ☎ 1438834

CAT NEXT DOOR... Terrific Tabby, sensuous, furry, striped, likes uptown and downtown. Seeks city cat for love, adventure, friendship, future. Must have positive attitude, no couch potatoes. ☎ 13126

DON'T WASTE YOUR MONEY on 1-900 CALL CAT lines! Call me direct! I'm hot and in heat! Outcalls only, Manhattan ☎ 472-0640

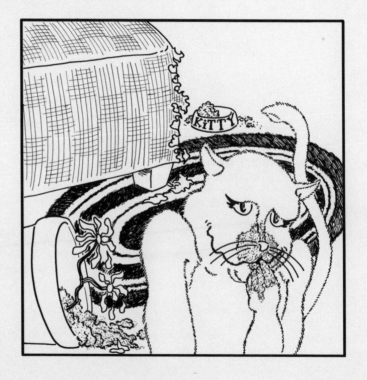

SPOILED ROTTEN I've always gotten everything I wanted, but not the old fashioned discipline I NEED... SFC desires MC for disciplinary sessions. No beginners. 88734

INNER CRAVINGS... STIRRING DESIRE
Warm connective bond... extremely intimate SFC, 8 lbs, full figured, pretty, sane, fem, ISO SFC 5-7, FEM, attractive, intelligent, funny, for genuinely moving experiences. Some messages lost last week, pls call again. ☎ 00876

SC PHOTOGENIC TABBY 4 yrs old, good jumper, declawed, no fear, seeks athletic SMC for house mate and family. 34567

OWNER NEEDED. Too old and tired for the singles scene... SFC almost 17, need fun loving young couple to take care of me. ☎ 14587

Siamese (w/papers) SFC, 12, but looks younger, slim 10 lbs, pure bred , seeks elegant high-class MC, well traveled, well bred. ✉ 61290

EX-MODEL CAT. FC seen on TV. 1997 Cat Fancy centerfold runner-up. Seeks down to earth MC, for slow-paced, honest relationship. No phonies pls. ✉ Send photo 61312

I HAVE A LOT TO GIVE. But I give it to the wrong cats. SMT very open & too honest for NYC. I don't use and abuse, would like to meet the same. UR profl, kind, mature SFC, 5-8, attractive both physically & mentally. lv mess. ☎ 89333

NEW TO THE CITY SFC born lonely, lost my playmate to pre-school, seeks friend for chasing around large apartment. Owners a bit crazy, but nice ☎ 13007

FC FILM BUFF, loves old Alfred Hitchcat film "The Birds"...Elizabeth Tailer in "Cat on a Hot Tin Roof," Woody Alleycat flicks...seeks "big daddy" MC to snuggle/share quiet nights with. Call ☎ 10003

FABIO LOOK-A-LIKE Distinctive nose, soft
eyes, chiseled face, untamed fur, long whiskers.
Likes fun, loves Hagen Daz, please call ☎
10067

Acrobatic, aqua-eyed angel, FC beauty wrapped in black mink can't get enough sleep, seeks MC to do the same. ☎ 11325

WHEN HAIRY MET CATTY. Commitment minded, caring, into poetree, diners, conversation, ISO romantic, spontaneous, caring cat for love afair. Status/breed irrelevant. ☎ 44505

Hi My name is FeeFee. I am very attractive. I have shiny black fur and weigh 4lbs. I like male cats who look like football players. If you are interested...give me a call. Uptown ☎ 938394

J LO LOOK ALIKE Sexy Bronx babe, SF Latino cat, 6 yo, olive complexion, athletic body, looking for bad boy/girl for cruising. Dress to impress. Manhattan ✉ 938395

MRS. ROBINSON TYPE Older, mature F cat seeks recent graduate (Ivy league only) for hot times. Columbia a +, Upper Eastside. ✉ 938396

BODELICIOUS LONG HAIR SEEKS GENTLEMAN. SF cat, 3 yo, ISO sexy, classy NPR buff. Must have a well padded couch and bank account. I'll scratch your back...you scratch mine. House in the Hampton's a must. Upper Eastside. ☎ 938397

CHICKEN LIVER DINNER... Saw you last Sunday about 4:00 at Balducci's. You recommended the sea food casserole...I said "The chicken liver was out of this world." You said "You'd like to try it." I said "How about my place?"...You purred, turned and rubbed your tail against my face and walked down to the dried food section. Can't stop thinking of you... Plse call Greenwich Village ☎ 938398

VERY FAT BLACK CAT 25 lbs, low maintenance, seeks no nonsense owner. 13990

LET'S ESCAPE... Healthy SMC, 5, never been outside except for going to the vet seeks SFC, young, daring for escapes to country living. I've got a plan... ☎ 13185

HOME ALONE MC well bred SWMC, 5, healthy, have all shots, no fleas, owner never home, for fun and games. ✉ 09021

VINCAT VAN GOGH... artist, lover, poet, dreamer, seeks inspiration, companionship, and truth. If you are artistic, sincere, honest, then my heart belongs to you. ✍ 08020

SFC, 10 LBS, 10" 2 years old. All the often-sought catly traits I possess, but I dream of that extra something of a male cat. Are you the one who can make me purr? ☎ Manhattan 13125

HAZEL EYED, VOLUPTUOUS, SFC, 8 lbs, 12" very youthful, would like to meet an emotionally secure country or city cat... You: witty, cute, romantic, No fleas please, breed unimportant. 13124

BURMESE REYNOLDS LOOK ALIKE My animal magnetism will make pussycats swoon... promiscuous puss, wanted for non-committal relationship. ☎ 08020

FJC Cuddly, creative, loving, optimistic, self-aware 5 y.o. non-smoking Jewish F cat seeks male cat of the same for family and fun. Note and photo please. ✉ 06711

NIP CRAZY, fun loving, SM tabby seeks SF tabby who likes to party til dawn. ☎ 45412

NYC BORN & BRED Owner moving to Texas. FC seeks home to stay in NYC. Declawed, well-behaved, affectionate. Good companion for elderly person. Good with kids ✉ 11121

BRAINS & BEAUTY Classical black SFC. Writing books for rich & poor. Needs inspirational Christian help. ☎ 09057

SUMMER SUN - SFC 8 lbs, 12" seeks sensual, slender kinda sub MC, 2-3 for naps, famiy and fun. Hampton Bays ✉ 11946-0607

CASTING A SPELL... Classic Blk Witch Cat
ISO companion... Lotions, potions and a dead
mouse tail, send me a love letter via express
mail. Tell me your magical, mystical and faith-
fully mine... I'll be yours 'til the end of time.
Hampton Bays ☎ 13088

Laid Back football loving M Cat seeks F cat for Monday night football extravaganzas. ☎ 13017

ASK & YOU SHALL RECEIVE... SFC seeks
Siamese, Burmese or Tabby M 2-5 years old
who can grant 3 wishes... in return for faithful
companion. ☎ 90854

CAT EYES WIDE SHUT Tomcat seeks sexy Nicole-ish female for masquerading around Manhattan. Must be open minded & affluent. Park Ave location preferred. lv message. ☎ 47826

GORGEOUS IN GRAMACY Career cat, sexy F Tabby, 4, 5lbs, petit, non-conformist seeks employed attractive M cat, must possess, wit, warmth, manners, (no throwing up hairballs or bothering my owner for food) Weekend fun only. Gramacy Park ☎ 47827

THE DOW...S & P 500 TURN YOU ON? Me too! Young M cat, 3 yo, clean and friendly, seeks mature corporate exec F cat for city fun. Brooks Bros. dress a +. You call the shots. Wall Street area ☎ 47828

PENN PLEASURES Long Island RR got you stressed? Unwind w. this hi-class female cat, 3 yo, wild looks, sweet temperament, experienced. You, well bred, affluent for mutual satisfaction. Discretion assured. lv message ☎ 47829

SEX KITTEN IN THE CITY Stunning, curvaceous F cat into trying new things, seeks prime time, prof. male cat for LTR. No strays or wierdo's. Clean cut only. Age, breed unimportant. Westside. ☎ 47830

I GOT ALL A'S Amiable, articulate, attractive athletic, alert, adventurous, artsy, affectionate, awesome SF cat. 5yo, desires downright handsome M cat, NS, flea free, for mice chasing, moon gazing and more. Possible LTR. Chelsea ✉ 47831

Looking for my common denominator
Affectionate, Friendly, SFC, audacious British
Blue w/papers, looks Upper East side, likes
Lower East Side, looking to find my common
denominator. U, eloquent, envolved, employed
and fertile. Note/photo pls. ✉ 33102

OPRAH ADDICT SFC Single mother seeks SMC to share dreams and watch TV w/VCR. (owner doesn't know that I know how to turn on TV) No strays or weirdos please. ☎ 90055

CLEOCATRA... Goddess from ancient times, tigress in the bedroom, I leave my lovers weak as kittens, ISO tom cats for ancient rituals. Wild cats only. 50004

SEARCHING FOR DOMESTIC BLISS? Great apartment! Newly renovated w/30" TV, TIVO cable, unlimited access to linen closet, overflowing bowls of cat food, challenging fire escape... and more. Must see to believe! Lonely SMC 5, 6 lbs, needs young SFC, shapely, disease free companion. Must have sweet temperament/people orientated. Lv message. ☎ 50036

ALL PURR, NO FUR. F sphynx, child adapted, can't get enough sleep, seeks MC to wile away the afternoons on sunny windowsills. 89008

ORGANIC HOLISTIC FC seeks MC to share natural living in stress free apartment... (owners are relatively stable NY couple) ☎ 11165

JE NE REGRETTE RIEN... Blue eyed, young, starry eyed, dreams of life in Paris... La vie en rose. Take me there for a day, a year, for eternity... rich romantics only. ✉ 06054

*VEGETARIAN** SMC seeks spiritual, organic holistic FC to share large Upper West Side apartment. Must love yoga and tofu. Searching for eternity...will you join me? ✉ 40045

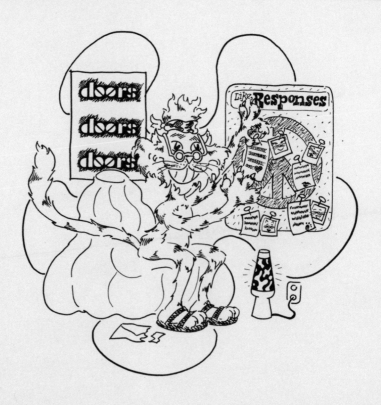

GROOVY! Bohemian. Upper West Side 60s tie-dyed MC loves The Doors and sound of rain, seeks cool FC to relive the 60s. ☎ 76934

LIVE IN NEEDED... SFC needed for light mousekeeping in fun loving family, warm home, roam free through fields and yards. Nice house, good neighborhood, great closets. Responsible, clean, references. Westchester ☎ 07020

PURRFECT MATCH F attractive, affectionate, seeks position in warm lap in exchange
for years of companionship. ✉ 10023

LIKEABLE, SOFT NM Persian Japanese cat, 5 years, 8 lbs, seeks partner of same. ✉ 67265

FOOT FETISH SFC seeks S&M owners who enjoy getting their feet bitten under the sheets. ☎ 00125

L.A. BASED INDEPENDENT OLDER MC 12 yrs old seeks young cat to remember what youth was like. Must be willing to relocate. ☎ 14222

Petite Parisian seeks mature American male for fun and resident card. 07170

The Classified Cat

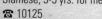

SBMC, 2 yrs old, all black, seeks disease free,
Siamese, 3-5 yrs. for meaningful relationship.
☎ 10125

SUN WORSHIPER Snowwhite outside but red hot inside...4 yo, 9 lbs, new to city, Libra, outgoing, fun, seeks attractive male for LTR. Overall I consider myself a female who loves life and continues to grow. Prefer similar style. ☎ 938399 Upper Westside

SIGNIFICAT OTHER NEEDED Mixed breed, MC, 3, Heavy set hippy, prof. ISO LTR w. outdoorsy, spiritual activist, looking to connect w.out the bs. Into "the Dead", Hendricks, Harley's. Hemp friendly. Age, race unimpoftant, NK, Will travel. ✉ Queens- 900469

I DON'T DO MORNINGS...so don't expect breakfast! Upscale, TS Siamese, into hard core club scene seeks sugar catty for hot nights & steamy afternoons. You, well endowed (in more ways than one) 10-17 y.o. with cat class and cat style. Possible menage trois w. friend. Will travel (exotic locations a +) Upper West side. call. ☎ 88450

Scratch my Itch...and I'll scratch yours... mature, Rubenesque D Ragdoll, in the mood for love ISO young stud muffin for hot times. You, clean (veterinarian certified a +) Declawed need not apply. Upper Eastside. lv mess. ☎ 88451

OUR EYES MET AT A BROOKLYN SUPER BOWL PARTY I can't find your phone no. anywhere. You, a small mouse... Patriots fan, me slender F cat...Cowboys fan. Opposites really do attract! Thinking of you. Call me...Manhattan. ☎ 88452

GREAT TONGUE Sexy SMBi Shorthair, 5 yo, I'm big into oral (but nobody I know is...) ISO open minded F/M cat for licking pleasure. No reciprocation. Satisfaction guaranteed. Be safe, clean, discreet. Uptown ☎ 88453

Hot M, 5 yo, Big Chill era, looking for blue eyed F Burmese for discreet safe + sane erotic fun. My strength and stamina will fulfill all your fantasies. Limits respected. Brooklyn. lv mess. ☎ 88454

COME SHARE THE SPRING AIR, just moved into a new apt. w/sunlight terrace. Great climbing, challenging fire escape... seeks friendly companion to share warmth of the sun. ✉ 10056